THE
ELDER BROTHER

John Fletcher
1579—1625

(From the Portrait at Welbeck Abbey, by permission of
his Grace the Duke of Portland)

THE
ELDER BROTHER

A COMEDY

BY

JOHN FLETCHER

First printed in 1637

Now reprinted with slight alterations and abridgement for
use on occasions of Entertainment especially
in Schools and Colleges

EDITED BY

WILLIAM H. DRAPER, M.A.

Cambridge :

at the University Press

1915

CAMBRIDGE
UNIVERSITY PRESS

University Printing House, Cambridge CB2 8BS, United Kingdom

Published in the United States of America by Cambridge University Press, New York

Cambridge University Press is part of the University of Cambridge.

It furthers the University's mission by disseminating knowledge in the pursuit of
education, learning and research at the highest international levels of excellence.

www.cambridge.org
Information on this title: www.cambridge.org/9781107426740

© Cambridge University Press 1915

First published 1915
First paperback edition 2014

A catalogue record for this publication is available from the British Library

ISBN 978-1-107-42674-0 Paperback

PREFACE

THE number of occasions for entertainment in the ever-developing life of our Universities, Colleges, and Schools, creates a demand for suitable plays or scenes, which has not met hitherto with an adequate supply.

John Fletcher's play *The Elder Brother*, which was first printed in 1637, seems well adapted for such occasions, for the following reasons.

(1) The gist of the play is to commend and praise learning by showing the character of A SCHOLAR as being not only consistent with patriotic and military prowess but as actually more favourable to these than the character of a mere courtier or popinjay. Although the tone of the play is pure comedy, the undertone is of weightier matter. It will be perhaps some recommendation that the scene is laid in France, a country more than ever knit to our own by recent history, and no English audience will be likely to miss the friendly allusion to the University of Louvain in Act II, Sc. 1.

(2) The characters of most importance are full of life and sparkle with wit, and are such as seem to 'put a spirit of youth in everything,' congenial to the occasions above mentioned.

(3) No elaborate scenery is required ; and, what is often of great consideration, it is possible to abbreviate the play and choose a few effective scenes and dialogues without entirely mutilating the general purpose of the whole.

There is only one woman character that has much to say and she is full of charm and good sense. Her maid Sylvia is a very good foil to her mistress, but is altogether of minor importance.

John Fletcher was a son of Richard Fletcher, Bishop of London (1594–1596), and it was to him and his brother Nathaniell that the Bishop bequeathed all his books 'to be devyded betweene them equallie.'

Though his name is inseparably linked with that of Francis Beaumont it is a generally accepted fact that the present play was entirely the work of Fletcher himself.

The lines, in the original edition, serving as prologue to Act I, as well as those which form the epilogue, testify to the great reputation in which the author was held, and the play itself was re-printed in 1651, 1661, 1678, in which year it is described as 'now being acted at the Theatre Royal by His Majesty's Servants.'

The Editor's thanks are due to His Grace the Duke of Portland for permission to reproduce the interesting portrait of Fletcher now at Welbeck, and to the Bishop of London for leave to photograph the monograms of Fletcher's father at Fulham.

W. H. D.

January 1915.

ILLUSTRATIONS

Arms of Richard Fletcher, the poet's father

NOTE

By the Rev. C. A. Alington,
Headmaster of Shrewsbury

EVERYONE who is interested in acting at Public Schools or Universities must have suffered from the dearth of suitable plays; and this fact alone should be enough to justify the re-publishing of this play by John Fletcher.

Besides this general merit it seems to me to have the special advantages claimed for it: the plot is simple and direct, the characters clearly drawn and the language remarkably free from difficulty.

We are often told that our countrymen despise learning, and pessimists maintain that the home life of the present day has degenerated from the beauty of the past. This play provides a cheerful antidote to both complaints: its moral is that of the supremacy of learning over ruder accomplishments,—a thesis which academic listeners must surely applaud: while if they are led to a comparison of modern domestic relations with those of the XVIIth century the result must certainly be to send them home content.

C. A. A.

January 1915.

THE ARGUMENT

A certain Lord, Lewis, thinks it is time his young daughter Angelina was married, and commends to her attention the two sons of his neighbour Brisac, a gentleman and Justice of the Peace, the elder of whom is Charles, a scholar and studious lover of books, and the younger Eustace, a soldier of fortune with certain vain fellows for friends. Brisac, who is no scholar, favours his younger son Eustace, but his brother Miramont, a lover of learning, favours Charles in his suit with Angelina, in which he is strongly aided by Charles' faithful servant Andrew. Angelina after much observation prefers Charles and awakens in him a generous passion. Thereupon Eustace and his friends aided by Brisac try to make Charles sign away his inheritance, but he boldly refuses and challenges Eustace to decide their claims by the sword. Eustace is so moved by admiration for his brother's courage that he resigns his claim to Angelina, who in the end is wedded to Charles.

Note. On occasions where it is necessary to present only a portion of the play, the following suggestions for abbreviation are offered.

SCHEME A. Act I, Sc. 1 and 2.

Act III, Sc. 2, to 'Get me my books again.' Sc. 4, to 'I must partake it with him.'

Act V, Sc. 1, and part of Sc. 2, from 'Well overtaken' to end.

SCHEME B. Act I, Sc. 1. Sc. 2, from 'Sir, my young masters are newly alighted' to end.

Act II, Sc. 2.

Act III, Sc. 2, to 'Get me my books again.'

SCHEME C. Act I, Sc. 1.

Act II, Sc. 1, to 'shows and sheriffs.'

Act III, Sc. 2, from 'Hark! hark! The coach that brings the fair lady' to end. Sc. 4, to 'Be't good or bad, I must partake it with him.'

THE
ELDER BROTHER,
A
COMEDY

Persons Represented in the Play

LEWIS, *a Lord.*

MIRAMONT, *a gentleman.*

BRISAC, *a Justice, brother to Miramont.*

CHARLES, *a scholar*
EUSTACE, *a courtier* } *sons to Brisac.*

EGREMONT
COWSY } *two courtiers, friends to Eustace.*

ANDREW, *servant to Charles.*

COOK
BUTLER } *servants to Brisac.*

PRIEST.

NOTARY.

SERVANTS.

OFFICERS.

ANGELINA, *daughter to Lewis.*

SYLVIA, *her woman.*

LILLY, *wife to Andrew.*

LADIES.

The Scene is laid in France

LECTORI

Would'st thou all Wit, all Comic Art survey ?
Read here and wonder ; Fletcher *writ the Play*

ACT I.

SCENE I. *A grove at some distance from the house of*
LEWIS.

Enter LEWIS, ANGELINA, *and* SYLVIA.

LEW. Nay, I must walk you farther.

ANG. I am tir'd, sir,
And ne'er shall foot it home.

LEW. 'Tis for your health ;
The want of exercise takes from your beauties,
And sloth dries up your sweetness : That you are
My only daughter and my heir, is granted ;
And you in thankfulness must needs acknowledge,
You ever find me an indulgent father,
And open handed.

ANG. Nor can you tax me, sir,
I hope, for want of duty to deserve
These favours from you.

LEW. No, my Angelina,
I love and cherish thy obedience to me,

I—2

Which my care to advance thee shall confirm :
All that I aim at, is to win thee from
The practice of an idle foolish state,
Us'd by great women, who think any labour
(Though in the service of themselves) a blemish
To their fair fortunes.

    ANG. Make me understand, sir,
What 'tis you point at.

    LEW. At the custom, how
Virgins of wealthy families waste their youth ;
After a long sleep, when you wake, your woman
Presents your breakfast, then you sleep again,
Then rise, and being trimm'd up by other hands,
You are led to dinner, and that ended, either
To cards or to your couch, (as if you were
Born without motion) after this to supper,
And then to bed : and so your life runs round
Without variety or action, daughter.

    SYL. Here's a learned lecture !

    LEW. From this idleness,
Diseases, both in body and in mind,
Grow strong upon you ; where a stirring nature,
With wholesome exercise, guards both from danger :
I'd have thee rise with the sun, walk, dance, or hunt
Visit the groves and springs, and learn the virtue
Of plants and simples : do this moderately,
And thou shalt not, with eating chalk, or coles,
Leather and oatmeal, and such other trash,
Fall into the green-sickness.

    SYL. With your pardon
(Were you but pleas'd to minister it) I could

Prescribe a remedy for my lady's health,
And her delight too, far transcending those
Your lordship but now mention'd.

LEW. What is it, Sylvia?

SYL. What is't! a noble husband; in that word,
A noble husband, all content of woman
Is wholly comprehended.

LEW. Well said, wench.

ANG. And who gave you commission to deliver
Your verdict, minion?

SYL. I deserve a fee,
And not a frown, dear madam: I but speak
Her thoughts, my lord, and what her modesty
Refuses to give voice to.

LEW. 'Tis well urg'd,
And I approve it: no more blushing, girl,
Thy woman hath spoke truth, and so prevented
What I meant to move to thee. There dwells near us
A gentleman of blood, Monsieur Brisac,
Of a fair estate, six thousand crowns *per annum*,
The happy father of two hopeful sons,
Of different breeding; the elder, a mere scholar;
The younger, a quaint courtier.

ANG. Sir, I know them
By public fame, though yet I never saw them;
And that oppos'd antipathy between
Their various dispositions, renders them
The general discourse and argument;
One part inclining to the scholar Charles,
The other side preferring Eustace, as
A man complete in courtship.

LEW. And which way
(If of these two you were to choose a husband)
Doth your affection sway you ?
   ANG. To be plain sir,
(Since you will teach me boldness) as they are
Simply themselves, to neither : let a courtier
Be never so exact, let him be bless'd with
All parts that yield him to a virgin gracious ;
If he depends on others,
Though he live in expectation
Of some huge preferment in reversion ; if
He want a present fortune, at the best
Those are but glorious dreams, and only yield him
A happiness in *posse*, not in *esse* ;
Nor can they fetch him silks from the mercer, nor
Discharge a tailor's bill, nor in full plenty
Maintain a family.
   LEW. Aptly consider'd,
And to my wish : but what's thy censure of
The scholar ?
   ANG. Troth (if he be nothing else)
As of the courtier, all his songs and sonnets,
His anagrams, acrostics, epigrams,
His deep and philosophical discourse
Of nature's hidden secrets, makes not up
A perfect husband ; he can hardly borrow
The stars of the celestial crown to make me
A tire for my head, nor Charles's Wain for a coach,
Nor Ganymede for a page, nor a rich gown
From Juno's wardrobe.
No, no, father

Though I could be well pleas'd to have my husband
A courtier, and a scholar, young, and valiant ;
These are but gawdy nothings, if there be not
Something to make a substance.

LEW. And what is that ?

ANG. A full estate, and that said, I've said all ;
And get me such a one with these additions,
Farewell singleness, and welcome wedlock.

LEW. But where is such a one to be met with,
daughter ?
A black swan is more common ; you may wear
Grey tresses ere we find him.

ANG. I am not
So punctual in all ceremonies, I will 'bate
Two or three of these good parts, before I'll dwell
Too long upon the choice.

SYL. Only, my lord, remember,
That he be rich and active, for without these,
The others yield no relish, but these perfect.
You must bear with small faults, madam.

LEW. Merry wench,
And it becomes you well ; I'll to Brisac,
And try what may be done.

> [*Exeunt, on one side*, ANGELINA *and* SYLVIA ; *on
> the other*, LEWIS.

SCENE II. *A room in the House of* BRISAC.

Enter ANDREW, COOK *and* BUTLER.

AND. Unload part of the library, and make room
For th'other dozen of carts ; I'll straight be with you.

COOK. Why, hath he more books ?

AND. More than ten marts send over.

BUT. And can he tell their names ?

AND. Their names ! he has 'em
As perfect as his *Pater Noster* ; but that's nothing,
H'as read them over leaf by leaf three thousand times ;
But here's the wonder, though their weight would sink
A Spanish galleon, without other ballast,
He carrieth them all in his head, and yet
He walks upright.

BUT. Surely he has a strong brain.

AND. If all thy pipes of wine were fill'd with books,
Made of the barks of trees, or mysteries writ
In old moth-eaten vellum, he would sip thy cellar
Quite dry, and still be thirsty : then for's diet,
He eats and digests more volumes at a meal,
Than there would be larks (though the sky should fall)
Devoured in a month in Paris. Yet fear not
Sons o'the buttery and kitchen, though his learn'd
  stomach
Cannot be appeas'd ; he'll seldom trouble you,
His knowing stomach contemns your black-jacks, butler,
And your flagons ; and Cook, thy boil'd, thy roast, thy
  bak'd.

COOK. How liveth he ?

AND. Not as other men do,
Few princes fare like him ; he breaks his fast
With Aristotle, dines with Tully, takes
His watering with the Muses, sups with Livy,
Then walks a turn or two in *Via Lactea*,
And (after six hours conference with the stars)
Sleeps with old *Erra Pater*.

BUT. This is admirable.

AND. I'll tell you more hereafter. Here's my old
    master,

And another old ignorant elder; I'll upon 'em.

Enter BRISAC, LEWIS.

BRI. What, Andrew? welcome; where's my
    Charles?

Speak, Andrew,

Where did'st thou leave thy master?

AND. Contemplating

The number of the sands in the high-way,

And from that, purposes to make a judgment

Of the remainder in the sea: he is, sir,

In serious study, and will lose no minute,

Nor out of's pace to knowledge.

LEW. This is strange.

AND. Yet he hath sent his duty, sir, before him

In this fair manuscript.

BRI. What have we here?

Pot-hooks and andirons!

AND. I much pity you,

It is the Syrian character, or the Arabic.

Would you have it said, so great and deep a scholar

As Mr Charles is, should ask blessing

In any Christian language? Were it Greek

I could interpret for you, but indeed

I'm gone no farther.

BRI. Take in the knave,

And let him eat.

AND. And drink too, sir

Bri.   And drink too sir,
And see your masters chamber ready for him.
  But.   Come, Dr Andrew, without disputation
Thou shalt commence i'the cellar.
  And.   I had rather
Commence on a cold bak'd meat.
  Cook.   Thou shalt ha't, boy.
                    [*Exeunt all except* Brisac *and* Lewis.
  Bri.   Good Monsieur Lewis, I esteem my self
Much honour'd in your clear intent, to join
Our ancient families, and make them one ;
And 'twill take from my age and cares, to live
And see what you have purpos'd but in act,
Of which your visit at this present is
A hopeful omen ; I each minute expecting
The arrival of my sons ; I have not wrong'd
Their birth for want of means and education,
To shape them to that course each was addicted ;
And therefore that we may proceed discreetly,
Since what's concluded rashly seldom prospers,
You first shall take a strict perusal of them,
And then from your allowance, your fair daughter
May fashion her affection.
  Lew.   Monsieur Brisac,
You offer fair and nobly, and I'll meet you
In the same line of honour ; and I hope,
Being blest but with one daughter, I shall not
Appear impertinently curious,
Though with my utmost vigilance and study,
I labour to bestow her to her worth :
Let others speak her form, and future fortune

From me descending to her; I in that
Sit down with silence.
  BRI. You may, my lord, securely,
Since fame aloud proclaimeth her perfections,
Commanding all men's tongues to sing her praises;
Should I say more, you well might censure me
(What yet I never was) a flatterer.
—What trampling's that without of horses?

Enter BUTLER.

  BUT. Sir, my young masters are newly alighted.
  BRI. Sir, now observe their several dispositions.
                             [Exit BUTLER
Enter CHARLES.

  CHAR. Bid my supsiser[1] carry my hackney to
The butt'ry, and give him his bever[2]; it is a civil
And sober beast, and will drink moderately;
And that done, turn him into the quadrangle.
  BRI. He cannot out of his university tone.

Enter EUSTACE, EGREMONT, COWSY.

  EUST. Lackey, take care our coursers be well rubb'd,
And cloth'd; they have out-stripp'd the wind in
      speed.
  LEW. Ay marry, sir, there's metal in this young
      fellow!
What a sheep's look his elder brother has!
  CHAR. Your blessing, sir.   *[Kneels.*
  BRI. Rise, Charles, thou hast it.

---

[1] i.e. underservant.   [2] i.e. drink.

EUST. Sir, though it be unusual in the court,
(Since 'tis the courtier's garb) I bend my knee,
And do expect what follows.   [*Kneels.*

BRI. Courtly begg'd.
My blessing, take it.

EUST. (*to* LEW.). Your lordship's vow'd adorer.
What a thing this brother is ! yet I'll vouchsafe him
The new Italian shrug
                    [*Aside : and then bows to* CHARLES.
How clownishly
The book-worm does return it !

CHAR. I'm glad you are well.
                [*Takes a book from his pocket and reads.*

EUST. Pray you be happy in the knowledge of
This pair of accomplish'd monsieurs ; they are gallants
That have seen both tropics.

BRI. I embrace their love.

EGR. Which we'll repay with servulating.

COW. And will report your bounty in the court.

BRI. I pray you make deserving use on't first.
Eustace, give entertainment to your friends ;
What's in my house is theirs.

EUST. Which we'll make use of ;
Let's warm our brains with half a dozen healths,
And then hang cold discourse, for we'll speak fire-works.
                [*Exeunt* EUSTACE, EGREMONT, *and* COWSY.

LEW. What, at his book already ?

BRI. Fie, fie, Charles,
No hour of interruption ?

CHAR. Plato differs
From Socrates in this.

BRI. Come, lay them by;
Let them agree at leisure.
CHAR. Man's life, sir, being
So short, and then the way that leads unto
The knowledge of our selves, so long and tedious,
Each minute should be precious.
BRI. In our care
To manage worldly business, you must part with
This bookish contemplation, and prepare
Your self for action; to thrive in this age
Is held the blame of learning; you must study
To know what part of my land's good for the
      plough,
And what for pasture; how to buy and sell
To the best advantage; how to cure my oxen
When they're o'er-done with labour.
CHAR. I may do this
From what I've read, sir; for, what concerns
      tillage,
Who better can deliver it than Virgil
In his *Georgics*? and to cure your herds,
His *Bucolics* is a masterpiece; but when
He does describe the commonwealth of bees,
Their industry, and knowledge of the herbs
From which they gather honey, with their care
To place it with *decorum* in the hive;
Their government among themselves, their order
In going forth, and coming loaden home;
Their obedience to their king, and his rewards
To such as labour, with his punishments
Only inflicted on the slothful drone;

I'm ravish'd with it, and there reap my harvest,
And there receive the gain my cattle bring me,
And there find wax and honey.

    BRI. And grow rich
In your imagination ; heyday, heyday !
Georgics, Bucolics, and bees ! art mad ?

    CHAR. No, sir, the knowledge of these guards me
        from it.

    BRI. But can you find among your bundle of books
(And put in all your dictionaries that speak all
        tongues)
What pleasure they enjoy, that do take home
A lovely wealthy bride ? Answer me that.

    CHAR. 'Tis frequent, sir, in story, there I read of
All kind of virtuous and vicious women ;
The ancient Spartan dames, and Roman ladies,
Their beauties and deformities ; and when
I light upon a Portia or Cornelia,
Crown'd with still flourishing leaves of truth and good-
        ness ;
With such a feeling I peruse their fortunes,
As if I then had liv'd, and freely tasted
Their ravishing sweetness ; at the present loving
The whole sex for their goodness and example.
But on the contrary, when I look on
A Clytemnestra, or a Tullia ;
The first bath'd in her husband's blood ; the latter,
Without a touch of piety, driving on
Her chariot o'er her father's breathless trunk,
Horror invades my faculties ; and comparing
The multitudes o'th' guilty, with the few

That did die innocents, I detest and loath 'em
As ignorance or atheism.
   BRI. You resolve then
Ne'er to make payment of the debt you owe me.
   CHAR. What debt, good sir?
   BRI. A debt I paid my father
When I married and made him a grandsire,
Which I expect from you.
   CHAR. The children, sir,
Which I will leave to all posterity,
Begot and brought up by my painful studies,
Shall be my living issue.
   BRI. Very well;
And I shall have a general collection
Of all the quiddits from Adam to this time,
To be my grandchild.
   CHAR. And such a one, I hope, sir,
As shall not shame the family.
   BRI. Nor will you
Take care of my estate?
   CHAR. But in my wishes;
For know, sir, that the wings on which my soul
Is mounted, have long since born her too high,
To stoop to any prey that soars not upwards.
Sordid and dunghill minds, compos'd of earth,
In that gross element fix all their happiness;
But purer spirits, purged and refin'd, shake off
That clog of humane frailty; give me leave
T'enjoy my self; that place that does contain
My books (the best companions) is to me
A glorious court, where hourly I converse

With the old sages and philosophers,
And sometimes for variety, I confer
With kings and emperors, and weigh their counsels,
Calling their victories (if unjustly got)
Unto a strict accompt, and in my fancy,
Deface their ill-plac'd statues ; can I then
Part with such constant pleasures, to embrace
Uncertain vanities ?   No, be it your care
T'augment your heap of wealth ; it shall be mine
T'increase in knowledge.   Lights there for my study !
                                                    [*Exit.*

   BRI.   Was ever man that had reason thus trans-
      ported
From all sense and feeling of his proper good ?
It vexes me, and if I found not comfort
In my young Eustace, I might well conclude
My name were at a period !
   LEW.   He is indeed, sir,
The surer base to build on.

Re-enter EUSTACE, EGREMONT, COWSY, *and* ANDREW.

   BRI.   Eustace.
   EUST.   Sir.
   BRI.   Your ear in private.
   AND. (*aside*).   I suspect my master
Has found harsh welcome, he's gone supperless
Into his study ; could I find out the cause,
It may be borrowing of his books, or so,
I shall be satisfied.
   EUST.   My duty shall, sir,

Take any form you please ; and in your motion
To have me married, you cut off all dangers
The violent heats of youth might bear me to.
  LEW. It is well answer'd.
  EUST. Nor shall you, my lord,
For your fair daughter ever find just cause
To mourn your choice of me ; the name of husband,
Nor the authority it carries in it,
Shall ever teach me to forget to be,
As I am now, her servant, and your lordship's ;
And but that modesty forbids, that I
Should sound the trumpet of my own deserts,
I could say my choice manners have been such,
As render me lov'd and remarkable
To the princes of the blood.
  COW. Nay, to the king.
  EGRE. Nay to the king and council.
  AND. (*aside*). These are court-admirers,
And ever echo him that bears the bag.
Though I be dull-ey'd, I see through this juggling.
  EUST. Then for my hopes.
  COW. Nay certainties.
  EUST. They stand
As fair as any man's. What can there fall
In compass of her wishes, which she shall not
Be suddenly possess'd of ? Loves she titles ?
By the grace and favour of my princely friends,
I am what she would have me.
  BRI. He speaks well,
And I believe him.
  LEW. I could wish I did so.   [*Aside.*

Pray you a word, sir. He's a proper gentleman,
And promises nothing, but what is possible.
So far I will go with you ; nay, I add,
He hath won much upon me ; and were he
But one thing that his brother is, the bargain
Were soon struck up.

    BRI. What's that, my lord ?

    LEW. The heir.

    AND. (*aside*). Which he is not, and I trust never
       shall be.

    BRI. Come, that shall breed no difference ; you
       see

Charles has given o'er the world ; I'll undertake,
And with much ease, to buy his birth-right of him
For a dry-fat of new books ; nor shall my state
Alone make way for him, but my elder brother's,
Who being issueless, to advance our name,
I doubt not will add his. Your resolution ?

    LEW. I'll first acquaint my daughter with the
       proceedings ;

On these terms I am yours, as she shall be,
Make you no scruple. Get the writings ready,
She shall be tractable ; to morrow we will hold
A second conference. Farewell noble Eustace ;
And you brave gallants.

    EUST. Full increase of honour
Wait ever on your lordship.   [*Exit* LEWIS.

    AND. (*aside*). The gout rather,
And a perpetual megrim.

    BRI. You see, Eustace,
How I travel to possess you of a fortune

You were not born to ; be you worthy of it :
I'll furnish you for a suitor : visit her,
And prosper in't.
    EUST. She's mine, sir, fear it not :
In all my travels, I ne'er met a virgin
That could resist my courtship. If it take now,
We're made for ever, and will revel it.
                        [*Exeunt all except* ANDREW.
    AND. In tough Welsh parsley, which, in our vulgar
        tongue,
Is strong hempen halters ; my poor master cozen'd,
And I a looker on ! If we have studied
Our majors and our minors, antecedents
And consequents, to be concluded coxcombs,
W'have made a fair hand on't. I am glad I have
        found
Out all their plots, and their conspiracies ;
This shall to old Monsieur Miramont, one, that though
He cannot read a proclamation,
Yet dotes on learning, and loves my master Charles
For being a scholar ;
I hear he's coming hither,
I shall meet him ; and if he be that old,
Rough, testy blade he always us'd to be,
I'll ring him such a peal, as shall go near
To shake their bell-room,
Peradventure beat 'em,
For he is fire and flax ; and so have at him. [*Exit.*

ACT II.

Scene I. *A room in* Brisac's *house.*

Enter Miramount, Brisac.

Mir. Nay, brother, brother.

Bri. Pray, sir, be not moved,
I meddle with no business but mine own,
And in mine own 'tis reason I should govern.

Mir. But how to govern then, and understand, sir,
And be as wise as you're hasty, though you be
My brother, and from one blood sprung, I must tell you
Heartily and home too.

Bri. What, sir?

Mir. What I grieve to find,
You are a fool, and an old fool, and that's two.

Bri. We'll part 'em, if you please.

Mir. No, they're entail'd to 'em.
Seek to deprive an honest noble Spirit,
Your eldest son, sir, and your very image,
(But he's so like you, that he fares the worse for't)
Because he loves his book, and dotes on that,
And only studies how to know things excellent,
Above the reach of such coarse brains as yours,
Such muddy fancies, that never will know farther
Than when to cut your vines, and cozen merchants,
And choke your hide-bound tenants with musty
      harvests?

Bri. You go too fast.

Mir. I'am not come to my pace yet.
Because h'has made his study all his pleasure,

And is retir'd into his contemplation,
Not meddling with the dirt and chaff of nature,
That makes the spirit of the mind mud too ;
Therefore must he be flung from his inheritance ?
Must he be dispossess'd, and Monsieur Gingle-boy[1]
His younger brother—

    Bri.   You forget your self.

    Mir.   Because h'has been at court, and learn'd new
        tongues,
And how to speak a tedious piece of nothing ;
To vary his face as sea-men do their compass,
To worship images of gold and silver,
And fall before the she-calves of the season ;
Therefore must he jump into his brother's land ?

    Bri.   Have you done yet, and have you spoke enough
In praise of learning, sir ?

    Mir.   Never enough.

    Bri.   But, brother, do you know what learning is ?

    Mir.   It is not to be a Justice of Peace as you are,
And palter out your time i'th' penal statutes.
To hear the curious tenets controverted
Between a Protestant constable, and Jesuite cobbler ;
Nor 'tis not the main moral of blind justice,
(Which is deep learning) when your worship's tenants
Bring a light cause, and heavy hens before ye,
Both fat and feeble, a goose or pig ;
And then you'll sit like equity with both hands
Weighing indifferently the state o'th' question.
These are your quodlibets, but no learning, brother.

---

[1] In Queen Elizabeth's time men wore boots with bells on their
spurs which thus jingled.

BRI. You are so parlously in love with learning,
That I'd be glad to know what you understand,
      brother;
I'm sure you have read all Aristotle.
   MIR. Faith no;
But I believe I have a learned faith, sir,
And that's it makes a gentleman of my sort;
Though I can speak no Greek, I love the sound of 't,
It goes so thund'ring as it conjur'd devils:
Charles speaks it loftily, and if thou wert a man,
Or had'st but ever heard of Homer's *Iliads*,
Hesiod, and the Greek poets, thou wouldst run mad,
And hang thy self for joy th' hadst such a gentleman
To be thy son: O he has read such things
To me!
   BRI. And you do understand 'em, brother?
   MIR. I tell thee, no, that's not material; the sound's
Sufficient to confirm an honest man:
Good brother Brisac, does your young courtier,
That wears the fine clothes, and is the excellent gentle-
      man,
(The traveller, the soldier, as you think too)
Understand any other power than his tailor?
Or knows what motion is more than an horse-race?
What the moon means, but to light him home from
      taverns?
Or the comfort of the sun is, but to wear slash'd clothes
      in?
And must this piece of ignorance be popt up,
Because 't can kiss the hand, and cry, sweet lady?
Must this thing therefore?—

BRI.   Yes sir, this thing must ;
I will not trust my land to one so sotted,
So grown like a disease unto his study ;
He that will fling off all occasions
And cares, to make him understand what state is,
And how to govern it, must, by that reason,
Be flung himself aside from managing.
My younger boy is a fine gentleman.
  MIR.   He is an ass, a piece of ginger-bread,
Gilt over to please foolish girls,—puppets.
  BRI.   You are my elder brother.
  MIR.   So I had need,
And have an elder wit, thou'dst shame us all else
Go to, I say, Charles shall inherit.
  BRI.   I say, no,
Unless Charles had a soul to understand it ;
Can he manage six thousand crowns a year
Out of the metaphysics ? or can all
His learn'd astronomy look to my vineyards ?
Can the drunken old poets make up my vines ?
(I know they can drink 'em) or your excellent humanists
Sell 'em the merchants for my best advantage ?
Can history cut my hay, or get my corn in ?
And can geometry vend it in the market ?
Shall I have my sheep kept with a Jacobs-staff now ?
I wonder you will magnifie this madman,
You that are old, and should understand.
  MIR.   Should, say'st thou ?
Thou monstrous piece of ignorance in office !
Thou that hast no more knowledge than thy clerk
        infuses,

Thy dapper clerk, larded with ends of Latin,
And he no more than custom of offences.
Thou unreprieveable dunce! that thy formal band-
    strings,
Thy ring, nor pomander cannot expiate for,
Dost thou tell me I should? I'll pose thy worship
In thine own library and almanac,
Which thou art daily poring on, to pick out
Days of iniquity to cozen fools in,
And full moons to cut cattle:
Dost thou taint me,
That have run over story, poetry, humanity?
  BRI. As a cold nipping shadow
Does o'er ears of corn, and leave 'em blasted,
Put up your anger, what I'll do, I'll do.
  MIR. Thou shalt not do.
  BRI. I will.
  MIR. Thou art an ass then,
A dull old tedious ass; th'art ten times worse
And of less credit than dunce Hollingshead
The Englishman, that writes of shows and sheriffs.

Enter LEWIS.

  BRI. Well, take your pleasure, here's one I must
    talk with.
  LEW. Good-day, sir.
  BRI. Fair to you, sir.
  LEW. May I speak wi'you?
  BRI. With all my heart, I was waiting on your
    goodness.
  LEW. Good morrow, Monsieur Miramont.

MIR. O sweet sir,
Keep your good morrow to cool your worship's
        pottage ;
A couple of the world's fools met together
To raise up dirt and dunghills.   [*Aside.*
    LEW. Are they drawn ?
    BRI. They shall be ready, sir, within these two
        hours ;
And Charles set his hand.
    LEW. 'Tis necessary ;
For he being a joint purchaser, though your estate
Was got by your own industry, unless
He seal to the conveyance, it can be
Of no validity.
    BRI. He shall be ready
And do it willingly.
    MIR. He shall be hang'd first.
                        [*Aside. Rises in anger.*
    BRI. I hope your daughter likes,
    LEW. She loves him well, sir ;
Young Eustace is a bait to catch a woman,
A budding spritely fellow ; you're resolv'd then,
That all shall pass from Charles ?
    BRI. All, all, he's nothing ;
A bunch of books shall be his patrimony,
And more than he can manage too.
    LEW. Will your brother
Pass over his land to your son Eustace ?
You know he has no heir.
    MIR. He will be flayed first,
And horse-collars made of's skin.

BRI.   Let him alone,
A wilful man ; my estate shall serve the turn, sir.
And how does your daughter ?
  LEW.   Ready for the hour,
And like a blushing rose that stays the pulling.
  BRI.   To morrow then's the day.
  LEW.   Why then to morrow
I'll bring the girl ; get you the writings ready.
  MIR.   But hark you, monsieur, have you the
      virtuous conscience
To help to rob an heir, an elder brother,
Of that which nature and the law flings on him ?
You were your father's eldest son, I take it,
And had his land ; would you had had his wit too,
Or his discretion, to consider nobly,
What 'tis to deal unworthily in these things ;
You'll say he's none of yours, he's his son ;
And he will say, he is no son to inherit
Above a shelf of books : Why did he get him ?
Why was he brought up to write and read, and know
      these things ?
Why was he not like his father, a dumb Justice ?
A flat dull piece of phlegm, shap'd like a man,
A reverend Idol in a piece of arras ?
Can you lay disobedience, want of manners,
Or any capital crime to his charge ?
  LEW.   I do not,
Nor do weigh your words, they bite not me, sir ;
This man must answer.
  BRI.   I have don't already,
And given sufficient reason to secure me :

And so good morrow, brother, to your patience.
  Lew. Good morrow, Monsieur Miramont.
                       [Exeunt Brisac *and* Lewis
  Mir. Good night-caps
Keep brains warm, or maggots will breed in 'em.
Well, Charles, thou shalt not want to buy thee books
        yet,
The fairest in thy study are my gift,
And the University of Louvain, for thy sake,
Hath tasted of my bounty ; and to vex
The old doting fool thy father, and thy brother,
They shall not share a solz of mine between them ;
Nay more, I'll give thee eight thousand crowns a year,
In some high strain to write my epitaph.

SCENE II. *Before the same house.*

Enter Eustace (*richly drest*), Egremont, Cowsy.

  Eust. How do I look now, compared to my elder
      brother ?
Nay, 'tis a handsome suit.
  Cow. All courtly, courtly.
  Eust. I'll assure you gentlemen, my tailor has
      travell'd,
And speaks as lofty language in his bills too ;
The cover of an old book would not shew thus.
Fie, fie ; what things these academics are !
These book-worms, how they look !
  Egre. They're mere images,
No gentle motion or behaviour in 'em ;
They'll prattle you of *primum mobile,*

And tell a story of the state of heaven,
What lords and ladies govern in such houses,
And what wonders they do when they meet together,
And how they spit snow, fire, and hail, like a juggler,
And make a noise when they are drunk, which we
　　call thunder.
　Cow.　They are the sneaking'st things, and the
　　contemptiblest ;
Such small-beer brains, but ask 'em any thing
Out of the element of their understanding,
And they stand gaping like a roasted pig :
Do they know what a court is, or a council,
Or how the affairs of Christendom are manag'd ?
Do they know any thing but a tired hackney ?
And they cry ' absurd ' as if the horse understood 'em.
They have made a fair youth of your elder brother,
A pretty piece of flesh !
　Eust.　I thank 'em for't,
Long may he study to give me his estate.
Saw you my mistress ?
　Egre.　Yes, she's a sweet young woman ;
But be sure you keep her from learning.
　Eust.　Songs she may have,
And read a little unbak'd poetry,
Such as the dabblers of our time contrive,
That has no weight nor wheel to move the mind,
Nor indeed nothing but an empty sound ;
She shall have clothes, but not made by geometry ;
Horses and coach, but of no immortal race :
I will not have a scholar in my house
Above a gentle reader ; they corrupt

The foolish women with their subtle problems;
I'll have my house call'd ignorance, to fright
Prating philosophers from entertainment.
  Cow. It will do well; love those that love good
      fashions,
Good clothes, and rich; they invite men to admire 'em,
That speak the lisp of Court. Oh 'tis great learning!
To ride well, dance well, sing well, or whistle courtly,
They're rare endowments. When are you marri'd?
  Eust. To morrow, I think; we must have a
      masque, boys,
And of our own making.
  Egre. 'Tis not half an hour's work,
A Cupid, and a fiddle, and the thing's done:
But let's be handsome, shall's be Gods or nymphs?
  Eust. What, nymphs with beards?
  Cow. That's true, we'll be knights then;
Some wand'ring knights, that light here on a sudden.
  Eust. Let's go, let's go, I must go visit, gentlemen,
And mark what sweet lips I must kiss to morrow.

ACT III.

Scene I. *A room in* Lewis's *house.*

Enter Lewis, Angelina, Sylvia, Notary.

  Lew. This is the day, my daughter Angelina,
The happy, that must make you a fortune,
A large and full one, my care has wrought it,
And yours must be as great to entertain it.

Young Eustace is a gentleman at all points,
And his behaviour affable and courtly,
His person excellent ; I know you find that,
I read it in your eyes, you like his youth ;
Young handsome people should be match'd together,
Then follow handsome children, handsome fortunes ;
The most part of his father's estate, my wench,
Is tied in a jointure, that makes up the harmony ;
And when you are married, he's of that soft temper,
And so far will be chain'd to your observance,
That you may rule and turn him as you please.
What, are the writings drawn on your side, sir ?

NOT.   They are, and here I have so fetter'd him,
That if the elder brother set his hand to,
Not all the power of law shall e'er release him.

LEW.   These notaries are notable confident knaves,
And able to do more mischief than an army.
Are all your clauses sure ?

NOT.   Sure as proportion ;
They may turn rivers sooner than these writings.

LEW.   Why did you not put all the lands in, sir ?

NOT.   'Twas not condition'd ;
If it had been found,
It had been but a fault made in the writing ;
If not found, all the land.

LEW.   These are small devils,
That care not who has mischief, so they make it ;
They live upon the mere scent of dissension.
'Tis well, 'tis well ; are you contented, girl ?
For your will must be known.

ANG.   A husband's welcome,

And as an humble wife I'll entertain him ;
No sovereignty I aim at, 'tis the man's, sir ;
For she that seeks it, kills her husbands honour :
The gentleman I have seen, and well observ'd him,
Yet find not that grac'd excellence you promise ;
A pretty gentleman, and he may please too,
And some few flashes I have heard come from him,
But not to admiration as to others :
He's young, and may be good, yet he must make it,
And I may help, and help to thank him also.
It is your pleasure I should make him mine,
And 't has been still my duty to observe you.

   LEW. Why then let's go, and I shall love your
      modesty.
[*To the servants within.*] To horse, and bring the
      coach out. Angelina,
To morrow you will look more womanly.

   ANG. So I look honestly, I fear no eyes, sir.

                              [*Exeunt.*

   SCENE II. *A hall in* BRISAC'S *house, with gallery
      into which* CHARLES' *study opens.*

Enter CHARLES *from his study with a book in his hand.*

   CHAR. What a noise is in the house ? my head is
      broken,
In every corner,
As if the earth were shaken with some strange collect,
There are stirs and motions. What planet rules this
      house ?

Enter ANDREW.

Who's there?

AND.   'Tis I, sir, faithful Andrew.

CHAR.   Come near, and lay thine ear down; hear'st
 no noise?

AND.   The Cooks
Are chopping herbs and mince-meat to make pies,
And breaking marrow-bones—

CHAR.   Can they set them again?

AND.   Yes, yes, in broths and puddings, and they
 grow stronger
For the use of any man.

CHAR.   What speaking's that?
Sure there's a massacre.

AND.   Of pigs and geese, sir,
And turkeys, for the spit.   The cooks are angry
 sirs,
And that makes up the medley.

CHAR.   Do they thus
At every dinner?   I ne'er mark'd them yet,
Nor know who is a cook.

AND.   They're sometimes sober,
And then they beat as gently as a tabor.

CHAR.   What loads are these?

   [*Servants cross the stage laden with viands.*

AND.   Meat, meat, sir, for the kitchen,
And stinking fowls the tenants have sent in;
They'll ne'r be found out at a general eating;
And there's fat venison, sir.

CHAR.   What's that?

AND.   Why deer,

Those that men fatten for their private pleasures,
And let their tenants starve upon the commons.

CHAR. I've read of deer, but yet I ne'er ate any.

AND. There's a fishmonger's boy with caviare, sir,
Anchovies, and potargo, to make you drink.

CHAR. Sure these are modern, very modern meats,
For I understand 'em not.

AND. No more does any man.

CHAR. And why is all this, prithee tell me, Andrew?
Are there any princes to dine here to day?
By this abundance sure there should be princes;
I've read of entertainment for the gods
At half this charge; will not six dishes serve 'em?
I never had but one, and that a small one.

AND. Your brother's married this day; he's married,
—Your younger brother Eustace.

CHAR. What of that?

AND. And all the friends about are bidden hither;
There's not a dog that knows the house, but comes too.

CHAR. Married! to whom?

AND. Why to a dainty gentlewoman,
Young, sweet, and modest.

CHAR. Are there modest women?
How do they look?

AND. O you'll bless yourself to see them.

        [*Charles throws down his books.*

(*Aside*) He parts with's books, he ne'er did so before
   yet.

CHAR. What does my father for 'em?

AND. Gives all his land,
And makes your brother heir.

CHAR. Must I have nothing?

AND. Yes, you must study still, and he'll maintain you.

CHAR. I am his eldest brother.

AND. True, you were so;

But he has leap'd o'er your shoulders, sir.

CHAR. 'Tis well;

He'll not inherit my understanding too?

AND. I think not; he'll scarce find tenants to let it out to.

CHAR. Hark! hark!

AND. The coach that brings the fair lady.

Enter LEWIS, ANGELINA, LADIES, NOTARY, *etc.*

AND. Now you may see her.

                                     [Looks out of window.

CHAR. Sure this should be modest,

But I do not truly know what women make of it,

Andrew; she has a face looks like a story,

The story of the heavens looks very like her.

AND. She has a wide face then.

CHAR. She has a cherubin's,

Cover'd and veil'd with modest blushes. Eustace,

Be happy, whiles poor Charles is patient.

Get me my books again, and come in with me—

                                     [Exeunt.

Enter BRISAC, EUSTACE, EGREMONT, COWSY, MIRAMONT.

BRI. Welcome, sweet daughter; welcome, noble brother;

And you are welcome, sir, with all your writings ;
Ladies, most welcome : what, my angry brother !
You must be welcome too, the feast is flat else.

MIR. I am not come for your welcome, I expect
none ;
I bring no joys to bless the pair withall ;
Nor songs, nor masques to glorify the nuptials ;
I bring an angry mind to see your folly,
A sharp one too, to reprehend you for it.

BRI. You'll stay and dine though.

MIR. All your meat smells musty,
Your table will shew nothing to content me.

BRI. I'll answer you here's good meat.

MIR. But your sauce is scurvy,
It is not season'd with the sharpness of discretion.

EUST. It seems your anger is at me, dear Uncle.

MIR. Thou art not worth my anger, th'art a boy,
A lump of thy father's lightness, made of nothing
But antic clothes and cringes ;
Look in thy head,
And 'twill appear a foot-ball full of fumes
And rotten smoke. Lady, I pity you ;
You are a handsome and a sweet young lady,
And ought to have a handsome man yok'd to you,
An understanding too ; this is a gimcrack,
That can show you nothing but new fashions ;
If he e'er have a child,
'Twill either prove a tumbler or a tailor.

EUST. These are but harsh words, uncle.

MIR. So I mean 'em.
Sir, you play harsher play wi' your elder brother.

EUST. I would be loth to give you—

MIR. Do not venture,

I'll make your wedding-clothes sit closer t'you then;
I but disturb you, I'll go see my nephew.

LEW. Pray take a piece of rosemary.

MIR. I'll wear it,

But for the lady's sake, and none of yours;
May be I'll see your table too.   [*Exit* MIRAMONT.

BRI. Pray do, sir.

ANG. A mad old gentleman.

BRI. Yes faith, sweet daughter,

He has been thus his whole age, to my knowledge;
He has made Charles his heir, I know that certainly;
Then why should he grudge Eustace any thing?

ANG. (*aside as she goes upstairs with ladies*).   I would
    not have a light head, nor one laden

With too much learning, as, they say, this Charles is,
That makes his book his mistress; sure there's some-
    thing

Hid in this old man's anger, that declares him
Not a mere sot.

BRI. Come, shall we go and seal, brother?

All things are ready, and the priest is here.
When Charles has set his hand unto the writings,
As he shall instantly, then to the wedding,
And so to dinner.

LEW. Come, let's seal the book first

For my daughter's jointure.

BRI. Let's be private in't, sir.

SCENE III. *Charles' study.*

Enter CHARLES, MIRAMONT, ANDREW.

MIR. Nay, you are undone.

CHAR. H'm.

MIR. Ha' you no greater feeling?

AND. You were sensible of the great book, sir,
When it fell on your head, and now the house
Is ready to fall, do you fear nothing?

CHAR. Will he have my books too?

MIR. No, he has a book,
A fair one too, to read on, and read wonders;
I would thou hadst her in thy study, nephew,
And 'twere but to new string her[1].

CHAR. Yes, I saw her,
And me thought 'twas a curious piece of learning,
Handsomely bound, and of a dainty letter.

AND. He flung away his book.

MIR. (*aside*). I like that in him;
Would he had flung away his dulness too,
And spoke to her.

CHAR. And must my brother have all?

MIR. All that your father has.

CHAR. And that fair woman too?

MIR. That woman also.

CHAR. He has enough then.
May I not see her sometimes, and call her sister?
I will do him no wrong.

---

[1] An allusion to the old way of fastening books with strings
instead of clasps.

MIR.   This makes me mad,
I could now cry for anger : these old fools
Are the most stubborn and the wilfullest coxcombs ;
Farewell, and fall to your book, forget your brother :
You are my heir, and I'll provide you a wife :
I'll look upon this marriage, though I hate it. [*Exit.*

Enter BRISAC.

BRI.   Where is my son ?
AND.   There, sir, casting a figure
What chopping[1] children his brother shall have.
   BRI.   He does well.   How do'st, Charles ?   still at
      thy book ?
   AND.   He's studying now, sir, who shall be his
      father.
   BRI.   Peace, you rude knave—come hither, Charles,
      be merry.
   CHAR.   I thank you, I am busy at my book, sir.
   BRI.   You must put your hand, my Charles, as I
      would have you,
Unto a little piece of parchment here :
Only your name ; you write a reasonable hand.
   CHAR.   But I may do unreasonably to write it.
What is it, sir ?
   BRI.   To pass the land I have, sir,
Unto your younger brother.
   CHAR.   Is't no more ?
   BRI.   No, no, 'tis nothing : you shall be provided
      for,
And new books you shall have still, and new studies,

[1] bonny-looking.

And have your means brought in without thy care, boy,
And one still to attend you.
  CHAR. This shews your love, father.
  BRI. I'm tender to you.
  AND. (*aside*). Like a stone, I take it.
  CHAR. Why father, I'll go down, an't please you let me,
Because I'd see the thing they call the gentlewoman;
I see no woman but through contemplation,
And there I'll do't before the company,
And wish my brother fortune.
  BRI. Do, I prithee.
  CHAR. I must not stay, for I have things above
Require my study.
  BRI. No, thou shalt not stay;
Thou shalt have a brave dinner too.
               [*Exeunt* BRISAC *and* CHARLES.
  AND. Now has he
O'erthrown himself for ever; I will down
Into the cellar, and be stark drunk for anger.   [*Exit.*

    SCENE IV. *A room in the same house.*

   Enter LEWIS, ANGELINA, EUSTACE, PRIEST,
    LADIES, COWSY, NOTARY, *and* MIRAMONT.

  NOT. Come, let him bring his son's hand, and all's done.
Is your's ready?
  PRI. Yes, I'll dispatch you presently,
Immediately, for in truth I am a hungry.
  EUST. Do, speak apace, for we believe exactly:

Do not we stay long, mistress ?

ANG. I find no fault,
Better things well done, than want time to do them.
Uncle, why are you sad ?

MIR. Sweet smelling blossom,
Would I were thine uncle to thine own content,
I'd make thy husband's state a thousand better,
A yearly thousand. Thou hast miss'd a man,
(But that he is addicted to his study,
And knows no other mistress than his mind)
Would weigh down bundles of these empty kexes.

ANG. Can he speak, sir ?

MIR. Faith yes, but not to women ;
His language is to Heaven, and heavenly wonder ;
To Nature, and her dark and secret causes.

ANG. And does he speak well there ?

MIR. O admirably !
But he's too bashful to behold a woman,
There's none that sees him, and he troubles none.

ANG. He is a man.

MIR. Faith yes, and a clear sweet spirit.

ANG. Then conversation me thinks—

MIR. So think I ;
But it is his rugged Fate, and so I leave you.

                  [*Kisses his hand to Angelina.*]

ANG. I like thy nobleness.

EUST. See my mad uncle
Is courting my fair mistress.

LEW. Let him alone ;
There's nothing that allays an angry mind
So soon as a sweet beauty : he'll come to us.

Enter BRISAC *and* CHARLES.

EUST.   My father's here, my brother too ! that's a
    wonder,
Broke like a spirit from his cell.
  BRI.   Come hither,
Come nearer, Charles ; 'twas your desire to see
My noble daughter, and the company,
And give your brother joy, and then to seal, boy ;
You do, like a good brother.
  LEW.   Marry does he,
And he shall have my love for ever for't.
Put to your hand now.
  NOT.   Here's the deed, sir, ready.
  CHAR.   No, you must pardon me a while, I tell you,
I am in contemplation, do not trouble me.
  BRI.   Come, leave thy study, Charles.
  CHAR.   I'll leave my life first ;
I study now to be a man, I've found it.
Before what man was, was but my argument.
  MIR. (*aside*).   I like this best of all. He has taken fire,
His dull mist flies away.
  EUST.   Will you write, brother ?
  CHAR.   No, brother, no ; I have no time for poor
    things,
I'm taking the height of that bright constellation.
  BRI.   I say you trifle time, son.
  CHAR.   I will not seal, sir ;
I am your eldest, and I'll keep my birth-right,
For Heaven forbid I should become example :
Had you only shew'd me land, I had deliver'd it,

And been a proud man to have parted with it ;
'Tis dirt, and labour.   Do I speak right, uncle ?
  MIR.   Bravely, my boy, and bless thy tongue.
  CHAR.   I'll forward :
But you have open'd to me such a treasure,
I find my mind free ; Heaven direct my fortune.
  MIR.   Can he speak now ? Is this a son to sacrifice ?
  CHAR.   Such an inimitable peace of beauty,
That I have studied long, and now found only,
That I'll part sooner with my soul of reason,
And be a plant, a beast, a fish, a fly,
And only make the number of things up,
Than yield to one foot of land, if she be tied to't.
  LEW.   He speaks unhappily.
  ANG.   And methinks bravely.
This the mere scholar ?
  EUST.   You but vex yourself, brother,
And vex your study too.
  CHAR.   Go you and study,
For 'tis time, young Eustace ; you want both man
      and manners ;
I've studied both, although I made no shew on't.
Go turn the volumes over I have read,
Eat and digest them, that they may grow in thee ;
Wear out the tedious night with thy dim lamp,
And sooner lose the day, than leave a doubt.
Distil the sweetness from the poets' spring,
And learn to love ; thou know'st not what fair is :
Traverse the stories of the great heroes,
The wise and civil lives of good men walk through ;
Thou hast seen nothing but the face of countries,

And brought home nothing but their empty words :
Why shouldst thou wear a jewel of this worth,
That hast no worth within thee to preserve her ?

[*To* ANGELINA.]

Beauty clear and fair,
    Where the air
Rather like a perfume dwells,
  Where the violet and the rose
  The blue veins in blush disclose,
And come to honour nothing else.

Where to live near,
    And planted there,
Is to live, and still live new ;
  Where to gain a favour is
  More than light, perpetual bliss,
Make me live by serving you

Dear again back recall
    To this light,
A stranger to himself and all ;
  Both the wonder and the story
  Shall be yours, and eke the glory ;
I am your servant and your thrall.

MIR. Speak such another ode, and take all yet.
What say you to the scholar now ?
  ANG. I wonder ;
Is he your brother, sir ?
  EUST. Yes, would he were buried ;
I fear he'll make an ass of me a younker[1].

---

[1] A younker is among sailors a boy employed in menial offices ;
cf. Falstaff, "What! will you make a younker of me?" *Henry IV*,
Pt. I, Act III, Sc. 3.

Ang.   Speak not so softly, sir, 'tis very likely.

Bri.   Come, leave your finical talk, and let's dispatch, Charles.

Char.   Dispatch, what ?

Bri.   Why the land.

Char.   You are deceiv'd, sir.

Now I perceive what 'tis that woos a woman,
And what maintains her when she's woo'd : I'll stop
     here.
A wilful poverty ne'er made a beauty,
Nor want of means maintain'd it virtuously :
Though land and moneys be no happiness,
Yet they are counted good additions.
That use I'll make ; he that neglects a blessing,
Though he want a present knowledge how to use it,
Neglects himself.   May be I have done you wrong,
     lady,
Whose love and hope went hand in hand together ;
May be my brother, that has long expected
The happy hour, and bless'd my ignorance ;
Pray give me leave, sir, I shall clear all doubts ;
Why did they shew me you ?   pray tell me that ?

    (Mir.   He'll talk thee into a pension for thy knavery.)

    Char.   You, happy you, why did you break unto
       me ?

The rosy sugr'd morn ne'er broke so sweetly :
I am a man, and have desires within me,
Affections too, though they were drown'd a while,
And lay dead, till the spring of beauty rais'd them ;
Till I saw those eyes, I was but a lump,
A chaos of confusedness dwelt in me ;

Then from those eyes shot love, and he distinguish'd,
And into form he drew my faculties ;
And now I know my land, and now I love too.
  BRI. We had best remove the maid.
  CHAR. It is too late, sir.
I have her figure here. Nay frown not, Eustace,
There are less worthy souls for younger brothers ;
This is no form of silk, but sanctity,
Which wild and wanton hearts can never dignify.
Remove her where you will, I walk along still,
For, like the light, we make no separation ;
You may sooner part the billows of the sea,
And put a bar betwixt their fellowships,
Than blot out my remembrance ; sooner shut
Old Time into a den, and stay his motion,
Wash off the swift hours from his downy wings,
Or steal eternity to stop his glass,
Than shut the sweet idea I have in me.
Room for an elder brother, pray give place, sir.
  MIR. (*aside*). H'as studied duel too ; take heed,
      he'll beat thee.
H'as frighted the old justice into a fever ;
I hope he'll disinherit him too for an ass ;
For though he be grave with years, he's a great baby.
  CHAR. Do not you think me mad ?
  ANG. No, certain, sir,
I have heard nothing from you but things excellent.
  CHAR. You look upon my clothes, and laugh at me,
My scurvy clothes !
  ANG. They have rich linings, sir.
I would your brother—

CHAR. His are gold and gawdy.

ANG. But touch 'em inwardly, they smell of copper.

CHAR. Can you love me ? I am an heir, sweet lady,
However I appear a poor dependent ;
Love you with honour, I shall love so ever.
Is your eye ambitious ? I may be a great man ;
Is't wealth or lands you covet ? my father must die.

    MIR. (*aside*). That was well put in, I hope she'll
        take it deeply.

CHAR. Old men are not immortal, as I take it ;
Is it you look for youth and handsomeness ?
I do confess my brother's a handsome gentleman,
But he shall give me leave to lead the way, lady.
Can you love for love, and make that the reward ?
The old man shall not love his heaps of gold
With a more doting superstition,
Than I'll love you. The young man his delights,
The merchant, when he ploughs the angry sea up,
And sees the mountain billows falling on him,
As if all the elements, and all their angers,
Were turn'd into one vow'd destruction,
Shall not with greater joy embrace his safety.
We'll live together like two vines,
Circling our souls and loves in one another,
We'll grow together, and we'll bear one fruit ;
One joy shall make us smile, and one grief mourn ;
One age go with us, and one hour of death
Shall shut our eyes, and one grave make us happy.

    ANG. And one hand seal the match, I'm yours for
        ever.

    LEW. Nay, stay, stay, stay.

ANG.   Nay certainly, 'tis done, sir.

BRI.   There was a contract.

ANG.   Only conditional,

That if he had the land, he had my love too ;

This gentleman's the heir, and he'll maintain it.

(*To Eustace.*)   Pray be not angry, sir, at what I say ;

Or if you be, 'tis at your own adventure.

You have the out-side of a pretty gentleman,

But by my troth your inside is but barren ;

'Tis not a face I only am in love with,

Nor will I say your face is excellent,

A reasonable hunting face to court the wind with ;

Nor they're not words, unless they be well plac'd too,

Nor your sweet dam-mes, nor your hired verses,

Nor telling me of clothes, nor coach and horses,

No nor your visits each day in new suits,

Nor your black patches you wear variously,

Some cut like stars, some in half-moons, some lozenges;

All which but shew you still a younger brother.—

MIR.   Gramercy, wench, thou hast a noble soul too.

ANG.   Nor your long travels, nor your little know-
     ledge

Can make me doat upon you.   Faith, go study,

And glean some goodness, that you may shew manly ;

Your brother at my suit I'm sure will teach you ;

Or only study how to get a wife, sir.

You are cast far behind, 'tis good you should be
     melancholy,

It shews like a Gamester that had lost his money ;

And 'tis the fashion to wear your arm in a scarf, sir,

For you have had a shrewd cut o'er the fingers.

Lew.   But are you in earnest ?

Ang.   Yes, believe me, father,
You shall ne'er choose for me ; you are old and dim, sir,
And th' shadow of the earth eclips'd your judgment[1].
You have had your time without control, dear father,
And you must give me leave to take mine now, sir.

Bri.   This is the last time of asking, will you set
     your hand to ?

Char.   This is the last time of answering, I will never.

Bri.   Out of my doors.

Char.   Most willingly.

Mir.   He shall, Jew,
Thou of the tribe of Man-y-asses, coxcomb,
And never trouble thee more till thy chops be cold,
     fool.

Ang.   Must I be gone too ?

Lew.   I will never know thee.

Ang.   Then this man will ; what fortune he shall
     run, father,
Be't good or bad, I must partake it with him.

                    [*Retire* Charles *and* Angelina.

                Enter Egremont.

Egre.   When shall the masque begin ?

Eust.   'Tis done already ;
All, all is broken off, I am undone, friend,
My brother's wise again, and has spoil'd all,
Will not release the land, has won the wench too.

Egre.   Could he not stay till the masque was past ?
     we are ready.

---

[1] S. T. Coleridge calls this one of the finest lines in our language.

What a scurvy trick's this?

Mir. O you may vanish,
Perform it at some hall, where the citizens wives
May see't for six-pence a piece, and a cold supper.
Come, let's go, Charles. And now, my noble daughter,
I'll sell the tiles of my house, e're thou shalt want,
    wench.
Rate up your dinner, sir, and sell it cheap:
Some younger brother will take't up in commodities.
Send you joy, nephew Eustace; if you study the law,
Keep your great pippin-pies, they'll go far with you.

Char. I'd have your blessing.

Bri. No, no, meet me no more.
Farewell, thou wilt blast mine eyes else.

Char. I will not.

Lew. Nor send not you for gowns.

Ang. I'll wear coarse flannel first.
        [*Exeunt Angelina, Charles, and Miramont.*

Bri. Come, let's go take some counsel.

Lew. 'Tis too late.

Bri. Then stay and dine; it may be we shall
    vex 'em.   [*Exeunt.*

ACT IV.

Scene I. *A Room in Brisac's House.*

Enter Brisac, Eustace, Egremont, Cowsy.

Brisac. Ne'er talk to me, you are no men but
        masquers;
Shapes, shadows, and the signs of men, court bubbles,
That every breath or breaks or blows away.
You have no souls, no metal in your bloods,

No heat to stir you when you have occasion :
Frozen dull things, that must be turn'd with levers.
Are you the courtiers, and the travell'd gallants ?
The spritely fellows that the people talk of ?
You have no more spirit than three sleepy sopes[1].

    EUST. What would you have me do, sir ?
    BRI. Follow your brother,
And get you out of doors, and seek your fortune.
Stand still becalm'd, and let an aged dotard,
A hair-brain'd puppy, and a bookish boy,
That never knew a blade above a pen-knife,
And how to cut his meat in characters,
Cross my design, and take thine own wench from thee,
In mine own house too ? Thou despis'd poor fellow !
    EUST. The reverence that I ever bare to you, sir,
Then to my uncle, with whom 't had been but sauciness
T' have been so rough—
    EGRE. And we not seeing him
Strive in his own cause, that was principal,
And should have led us on, thought it ill manners
To begin a quarrel here.
    BRI. You dare do nothing.
Do you make your care the excuse of your cowardice ?
Three boys on hobby-horses, with three penny halberds,
Would beat you all.
    COW. You must not say so.
    BRI. Yes,
And sing it too.
    COW. You are a man of peace,
Therefore we must give way.

[1] Sots.

BRI.   I'll make my way,
And therefore quickly leave me, or I'll force you;
And having first torn off your flanting feathers,
I'll trample on 'em; and if that cannot teach you
To quit my house, I'll kick you out of my gates;
You gawdy glow-worms, carrying seeming fire,
Yet have no heat within you.

Cow.   O blest travel!
How much we owe thee for our power to suffer!

EGRE.   Some splenitive youths now, that had never
    seen
More than thy country smoke, will grow in choler;
It would shew fine in us.

EUST.   Yes marry would it,
That are prime courtiers, and must know no angers,
But give thanks for our injuries, if we purpose
To hold our places.

BRI.   Will you find the door?
And find it suddenly?
You shall lead the way, sir,
With your perfum'd retinue, and recover
The now lost Angelina, or build on it,
I will adopt some beggar's doubtful issue,
Before thou shalt inherit.

EUST.   We'll to counsel,
And what may be done by man's wit or valour,
We'll put in execution.

BRI.   Do, or never
Hope I shall know thee.   [*Exeunt.*

SCENE II.   *A Room in house of Miramont with balcony.*

Enter ANGELINA, CHARLES, SYLVIA *with a taper.*

ANG.   I must be gone.

CHAR.   Do not, I will not hurt you;
This is to let you know, my worthiest lady,
You have clear'd my mind, and I can speak of love too:
Fear not my manners, though I never knew,
Before these few hours, what a beauty was,
And such a one that fires all hearts that feel it;
Yet I have read of virtuous temperance,
And studied it among my other secrets;
And sooner would I force a separation
Betwixt this spirit and the case of flesh,
Than but conceive one rudeness against thee.

ANG.   Then we may walk.

CHAR.   And talk of any thing,
I am no courtier of a light condition,
Apt to take fire at every beauteous face;
That only serves his will and wantonness,
And lets the serious part run by
As thin neglected sand.   Whiteness of name,
You must be mine; why should I rob my self
Of that that lawfully must make me happy?
We'll lose our selves in Venus groves of myrtle,
Where every little bird shall be a Cupid,
And sing of love and youth.   Each wind that blows,
And curls the velvet-leaves, shall breed delights,
The wanton springs shall call us to their banks,
And on the perfum'd flowers we'll feast our senses;
Yet we'll walk by untainted of their pleasures,

And as they were pure temples we'll talk in them.

ANG. (*as they are parting*) Good night. Pray then,
we may have a fair end
Of our fair loves ; would I were worthy of you,
Or of such parents that might give you thanks :
But I am poor in all but in your love.
Once more, good night.

CHAR. A good night t'you, and may
The dew of sleep fall gently on you, sweet one,
And lock up those fair lights in pleasing slumbers ;
No dreams but chaste and clear attempt your fancy,
And break betimes sweet morn, I've lost my light else.

ANG. Let it be ever night when I lose you.

SYL. This scholar never went to a free-school, he's
so simple.

Enter a SERVANT.

SERV. Your brother, with two gallants, is at door,
sir,
And they're so violent, they'll take no denial

ANG. This is no fit time of night.

CHAR. Let 'em in, mistress.

SERV. They stay no leave ; shall I raise the house
on 'em ?

CHAR. Not a man, nor make no murmur of't I
charge you.

Enter EUSTACE, EGREMONT, COWSY.

EUST. They're here, my uncle absent, stand close
to me.
How do you, brother, with your curious story ?

Have you not read her yet sufficiently ?

CHAR.   No, brother, no ; I stay yet in the preface :
The style's too hard for you.

EUST.   I must entreat her ;
She's parcel of my goods.

[*Attempts to seize Angelina.*

CHAR.   She's all when you have her.

ANG.   Hold off your hands, unmannerly, rude sir ;
Nor I, nor what I have depend on you.

CHAR.   Do, let her alone, she gives good counsel :
    do not
Trouble your self with ladies, they are too light :
Let out your land, and get a provident steward.

ANG.   I cannot love you, let that satisfy you ;
Such vanities as you, are to be laugh'd at.

EUST.   Nay, then you must go ; I must claim
    mine own.   [*Again tries to seize Angelina.*

EGRE.⎫
COW. ⎬   Away, away with her !

CHAR.   Let her alone,

[*She strikes off Eustace's hat.*

Pray let her alone, and take your coxcomb up :
Let me talk civilly a while with you, brother.
It may be on some terms I may part with her.

EUST.   O, is your heart come down ? what are
    your terms, sir ?
Put up, put up.   [*To Egremont and Cowsy.*

CHAR.   This is the first and chiefest ;
[*Snatches away his sword*] let's walk a turn.
Now stand off, fools, I advise you,
Stand as far off as you would hope for mercy :

This is the first sword yet I ever handled,
And a sword's a beauteous thing to look upon ;
And if it hold, I shall so hunt your insolence :
'Tis sharp, I'm sure, and if I put it home,
'Tis ten to one I shall new pink your satins ;
I find I have spirit enough to dispose of it,
And will enough to make you all examples ;
Let me toss it round, I have the full command on't.
Fetch me a native fencer, I defy him ;
I feel the fire of ten strong spirits in me.
Do you watch me when my uncle is absent ?
This is my grief, I shall be flesh'd on cowards ;
Teach me to fight, I willing am to learn.
Are ye all gilded flies, nothing but shew in you ?
Why stand you gaping ?
Who now touches her ?
Who calls her his, or who dares name her to me ?
But name her as his own ; who dares look on her ?
That shall be mortal too ; but think, 'tis dangerous.
Art thou a fit man to inherit land,
And hast no wit nor spirit to maintain it ?
Stand still, thou sign of a man, and pray for thy friends,
Pray heartily, good prayers may restore you.
   ANG. But do not kill 'em, sir.
   CHAR. You speak too late, dear ;
It is my first fight, and I must do bravely,
I must not look with partial eyes on any ;
I cannot spare a button of these gentlemen ;
Did life lie in their heel, Achilles like,
I'd shoot my anger at those parts, and kill 'em.
Who waits within ?

Enter SERVANT.

SER. Sir.

CHAR. View all these, view 'em well,
Go round about 'em, and still view their faces ;
Round about yet, see how death waits upon 'em,
For thou shalt never view 'em more.

EUST. Pray hold, sir.

CHAR. I cannot hold, you stand so fair before me ;
I must not hold ; 'twill darken all my glories.
Go to my uncle, bid him post to the king,
And get my pardon instantly, I have need on't.

EUST. Are you so unnatural ?

CHAR. You shall die last, sir,
I'll take thee dead, thou art no man to fight with.
Come, will ye come ?   Me-thinks I've fought whole
        battles.

COW. We have no quarrel to you that we know on, sir.

EGRE. We'll quit the house, and ask ye mercy too.
Good lady, let no murther be done here ;
We came but to parley.

CHAR. How my sword
Thirsts after them !   Stand away, sweet.

EUST. Pray, sir, take my submission, and I dis-
        claim for ever.

CHAR. Away, you poor things, you despicable
        creatures !
Do you come post to fetch a lady from me ?
From a poor schoolboy that you scorn'd of late,
And grow lame in your hearts when you should execute ?
Pray take her, take her, I am weary of her :
What did you bring to carry her ?

EGRE. A coach and four horses.

CHAR. But are they good ?

EGRE. As good as France can shew sir.

CHAR. Are you willing to leave those, and take
   your safeties ?

Speak quickly.

EUST. Yes with all our hearts.

CHAR. 'Tis done then.

Many have got one horse, I've got four by th' bargain.

Enter MIRAMONT.

MIR. How now, who's here ?

SER. Nay, now you are gone without bail.

MIR. What, drawn, my friends ? Fetch me my
   two-hand sword ;

I will not leave a head on your shoulders, wretches.

EUST. In troth, sir, I came but to do my duty.

EGRE.⎫
Cow. ⎭ And we to renew our loves.

MIR. Bring me a blanket.

What came they for ?

ANG. To borrow me a while, sir ;

But one that never fought yet, has so curried,

So bastinado'd them with manly carriage,

They stand like things Gorgon had turn'd to stone :

They watch'd your being absent, and then thought

They might do wonders here, and they have done so ;

For by my troth I wonder at their coldness,

The nipping north or frost never came near them ;

St George upon a sign would grow more sensible.

If the name of honour were for ever to be lost,

These were the most sufficient men to do it
In all the world ; and yet they are but young,
What will they rise to ? They're as full of fire
As a frozen glow-worms rattle, and shine as goodly :
Nobility and patience are match'd rarely
In these three gentlemen, they have right use on't ;
They'll stand still for an hour and be beaten.
These are the anagrams of three great worthies.

   MIR.   They will infect my house with cowardice,
If they breathe longer in it ; my roof covers
No baffled monsieurs, walk and air your selves ;
As I live they stay not here.   White-liver'd wretches,
Without one word to ask a reason why.
Vanish, 'tis the last warning, and with speed ;
For if I take you in hand, I shall dissect you,
And read upon your phlegmatic dull carcases.
My horse again there : I have other business,
Which you shall hear hereafter, and laugh at it.
Good-night Charles, fair goodness to your dear lady ;
'Tis late, 'tis late.

       [*Leads Angelina off to door at centre back.*
   ANG.   Pray, sir, be careful of us.
   MIR.   It is enough, my best care shall attend you.
                           [*Exeunt.*

ACT V.

SCENE I.   *A Grove before Miramont's House.*

Enter EUSTACE, EGREMONT, COWSY.

   EUST.   Turn'd out of doors and baffled !
   EGRE.   We share with you
In the affront.

Cow. Yet bear it not like you
With such dejection.

Eust. My coach and horses made
The ransom of our cowardice !

Cow. Pish, that's nothing,
'Tis *damnum reparabile*, and soon recover'd.

Egre. It is but feeding a suitor with false hopes,
And after squeeze him with a dozen of oaths,
You are new rigg'd, and this no more remembered.

Eust. And does the court,
That should be the example and oracle of the kingdom,
Read to us no other doctrine ?

Egre. None that thrives so well as that,
Within my knowledge.

Cow. Flattery rubs out ;
But since great men learn to admire themselves,
'Tis something crest-fallen.

Egre. To be of no religion, argues a subtle,
Moral understanding, and it is often cherish'd.

Eust. Piety then, and valour,
Nor to do and suffer wrong,—
Are they no virtues ?

Egre. Rather vices, Eustace ;
Fighting ! what's fighting ?
It may be in fashion among provant swords,
And buff-jerkin men :
But with us that swim in choice of silks and tissues,
Though in defence of that word reputation,
Which is indeed a kind of glorious nothing,
To lose a dram of blood must
Needs appear as coarse as to be honest.

Eust.   And all this you seriously believe ?

Cow.   It is a faith that we will die in, since
From the black guard to the grim sir in office,
There are few hold other tenets.

Eust.   Now my eyes are open,
And I behold a strong necessity
That keeps me knave and coward.

Cow.   You are the wiser.

Eust.   Nor can I change my copy, if I purpose
To be of your society.

Egre.   By no means.

Eust.   Honour is nothing with you ?

Cow.   A mere bubble ;
For what's grown common, is no more regarded.

Eust.   My sword forc'd from me too, and still
    detain'd,
You think 'tis no blemish.

Egre.   Get me a baton,
'Tis twenty times more courtlike, and less trouble.

Eust.   And yet you wear a sword.

Cow.   Yes, and a good one,
A Milan hilt and a Damasco blade
For ornament, not use, the court allows it.

Eust.   Will't not fight of it self ?

Cow.   I ne'er tri'd this,
Yet I have worn as fair as any man ;
I'm sure I've made my cutler rich, and paid
For several weapons, Turkish and Toledo's,
Two thousand crowns, and yet could never light
Upon a fighting one.

Eust.   I'll borrow this,

I like it well.

Cow. 'Tis at your service, sir,
A lath in a velvet scabbard will serve my turn.

Eust. And now I have it, leave me; you are infectious,
The plague and leprosy of your baseness spreading
On all that do come near you ; such as you
Render the throne of majesty, the court,
Suspected and contemptible.

Egre. What sudden rapture's this ?

Eust. A heavenly one, that raising me from sloth
    and ignorance,
(In which your conversation long hath charm'd me)
Carries me up into the air of action,
And knowledge of my self ; even now I feel,
But pleading only in the court's defence
(Though far short of her merits and bright lustre)
A happy alteration, and full strength
To stand her champion against all the world,
That throw aspersions on her.

Cow. Sure he'll beat us,
I see it in his eyes.

Egre. A second Charles ;
Pray look not, sir, so furiously.

Eust. Recant
What you have said, you Mongrels, and take back
The shame you have cast upon the court,
Where you unworthily have had warmth and breeding,
And swear that you, like spiders, have made poison
Of that which was a saving antidote.

Egre. We will swear any thing.

Cow. We honour the court

As a most sacred place.

EGRE. And will make oath,
If you enjoin us to't, nor knave, nor fool,
Nor coward living in it.

EUST. Except you two,
You rascals.

COW. Yes, we are all these, and more,
If you will have it so.

EUST. And that until
You are again reform'd and grown new men,
You ne'er presume to name the court, or press
Into the porter's lodge but for a penance,
To be disciplin'd for your roguery, and this done
With true contrition.

BOTH. Yes, sir.

EUST. You again
May eat scraps, and be thankful.

COW. Here's a cold breakfast
After a sharp night's walking.

EUST. Keep your oaths,
And without grumbling vanish.

BOTH. We are gone, sir.   [*Exeunt.*

EUST. May all the poorness of my spirit go with
        you :
The fetters of my thraldom are fil'd off,
And I at liberty to right my self ;
And though my hope in Angelina's little,
My honour (unto which compar'd she's nothing)
Shall, like the sun, disperse those low'ring clouds
That yet obscure and dim it ; not the name
Of brother shall divert me, but from him,

That in the world's opinion ruin'd me,
I will seek reparation, and call him
Unto a strict accompt. Ha! 'tis near day,
And if the muses' friend, rose-cheek'd Aurora,
Invite him to this solitary grove,
As I much hope she will, he seldom missing
To pay his vows here to her, I shall hazard
To hinder his devotions—the door opens,
'Tis he most certain, and by's side my sword.
Blest opportunity!

Enter CHARLES.

CHAR. I have o'er-slept my self,
And lost part of the morn, but I'll recover it:
Before I went to bed, I wrote some notes
Within my table-book, which I will now consider.
Ha! what means this? What do I with a sword?
Learn'd Mercury needs not th' aid of Mars, and inno-
    cence
Is to it self a guard; yet since arms ever
Protect arts, I may justly wear and use it;
For since 'twas made my prize, I know not how
I'm grown in love with't, and cannot eat nor study,
And much less walk without it. But I trifle,
Matters of more weight ask my judgment.
EUST. Now, Sir,
Treat of no other theme, I'll keep you to it,
And see you expound it well.
CHAR. Eustace!
EUST. The same, sir,
Your younger brother, who, as duty binds him,

Hath all this night (turn'd out of door) attended,
To bid good-morrow t'you.

    CHAR. This, not in scorn,
Commands me to return it. Would you ought else ?

    EUST. O much, sir, here I end not, but begin ;
I must speak to you in another strain
Than yet I ever us'd ; and if the language
Appear in the delivery rough and harsh,
You (being my tutor) must condemn your self,
From whom I learn'd it.

    CHAR. When I understand
(Be't in what style you please) what's your demand,
I shall endeavour, in the self-same phrase,
To make an answer to the point.

    EUST. I come not
To lay claim to your birth-right, 'tis your own,
And 'tis fit you enjoy it ; nor ask I from you
Your learning and deep knowledge ; (though I am not
A scholar as you are) I know them diamonds
By your sole industry, patience and labour,
Forc'd from steep rocks, and with much toil attended,
And but to few that prize their value granted,
And therefore without rival freely wear them.

    CHAR. These not repin'd at (as you seem t'inform
      me)
The motion must be of a strange condition,
If I refuse to yield to't ; therefore, Eustace,
Without this tempest in your looks, propound it,
And fear not a denial.

    EUST. I require then
(As from an enemy, and not a brother)

The reputation of a man, the honour,
Not by a fair war won when I was waking,
But in my sleep of folly ravish'd from me ;
With these, the restitution of my sword,
With large acknowledgment of satisfaction,
My coach, my horses ; I will part with life,
Ere lose one hair of them ; and, what concludes all,
My mistress Angelina, as she was
Before the musical magic of thy tongue
Enchanted and seduc'd her. These perform'd,
And with submission, and done publicly,
At my father's and my uncle's intercession,
(That I put in too,) I perhaps may listen
To terms of reconcilement ; but if these,
In every circumstance, are not subscrib'd to,
To the last gasp I defy thee.
  CHAR. These are strict
Conditions to a brother.
  EUST. My rest is up,
Nor will I give less.
  CHAR. I'm no gamester, Eustace,
Yet I can guess your resolution stands
To win or lose all ; I rejoice to find you
Thus tender of your honour, and that at length
You understand what a wretched thing you were,
How deeply wounded by your self, and made
Almost incurable in your own hopes,
The dead flesh of pale cowardice growing over
Your fester'd reputation, which no balm
Or gentle unguent could ever make way to ;
And I am happy that I was the surgeon

That did apply those burning corrosives,
That render you already sensible
O'th' danger you were plung'd in, in teaching you,
And by a fair gradation, how far,
And with what curious respect and care
The peace and credit of a man within,
(Which you ne'er thought till now) should be preferr'd
Before a gaudy outside ; pray you fix here,
For so far I go with you.

   EUST.   This discourse
Is from the subject.

   CHAR.   I'll come to it, brother ;
But if you think to build upon my ruins,
You'll find a false foundation : your high offers,
Taught by the masters of dependencies,
That by compounding differences 'tween others,
Supply their own necessities, with me
Will never carry't : as you are my brother,
I will dispense a little, but no more
Than honour can give way to ; nor must I
Destroy that in my self I love in you ;
And therefore let not hopes or threats persuade you
I will descend to any composition
For which I may be censur'd.

   EUST.   You shall fight then.

   CHAR.   With much unwillingness with you ; but if
There's no evasion—

   EUST.   None.

   CHAR.   Hear yet a word ;
As for the sword and other fripperies,
In a fair way send for them, you shall have 'em.

But rather than surrender Angelina,
Or hear it again mention'd, I oppose
My breast unto loud thunder, cast behind me
All ties of nature.

 Eust. She detain'd, I'm deaf
To all persuasion.

 Char. Guard thy self then, Eustace ;
I use no other rhetoric.

Enter Miramont.

 Mir. Clashing of swords
So near my house ! Brother oppos'd to brother !
Here's no fencing at half sword ; hold, hold,
Charles, Eustace.

 Eust. Second him, or call in more help.
Come not between us, I'll not know nor spare you ;
D'you fight by th' book ?

 Char. 'Tis you that wrong me, off sir,
And suddenly, I'll conjure down the spirit
That I have rais'd in him.

 Eust. Never, Charles,
'Tis thine, and in thy death, be doubled in me.

 Mir. I'm out of breath, yet trust not too much to't,
  boys ;
For if you pause not suddenly, and hear reason,
Do, kill your uncle, do ; but that I'm patient,
And not a choleric old testy fool,
Like your father, I'd dance a matachin[1] with you,
Should make you sweat your best blood for't ; I would,
And it may be I will.

    [1] A military dance

Charles, I command thee,
And Eustace, I entreat thee, th'art a brave spark,
A true tough-metall'd blade, and I begin
To love thee heartily ; give me a fighting courtier,
I'll cherish him for example ; in our age
They're not born every day.
    CHAR.   You of late, sir,
In me lov'd learning.
    MIR.   True, but take me with you, Charles ;
'Twas when young Eustace wore his heart in's breeches,
And fought his battles in compliments and cringes,
When his understanding wav'd in a flaunting feather,
And his best contemplation look'd no further
Than a new fashion'd doublet ; I confess then,
The lofty noise your Greek made, only pleas'd me ;
But now he's turn'd an Oliver and a Roland,
Nay, the whole dozen of peers are bound up in him :
Let me remember, when I was of his years,
I did look very like him ; and did you see
My picture as I was then, you would swear
That gallant Eustace (I mean, now he dares fight)
Was the true substance, and the perfect figure.
Nay, nay, no anger, you shall have enough, Charles.
    CHAR.   Sure, sir, I shall not need addition from him.
    EUST.   Nor I from any, this shall decide my interest ;
Though I am lost to all deserving men,
To all that men call good, for suffering tamely
Insufferable wrongs, and justly slighted
By yielding to a minute of delay
In my revenge, and from that made a stranger
Unto my father's house and favour, o'erwhelm'd

With all disgraces ; yet I will mount upward,
And force my self a fortune, though my birth
And breeding do deny it.

CHAR. Seek not, Eustace,
By violence, what will be offer'd to you
On easier composition ; though I was not
Allied unto your weakness, you shall find me
A brother to your bravery of spirit,
And one that, not compell'd to't by your sword,
(Which I must never fear) will share with you
In all but Angelina.

MIR. Nobly said, Charles,
And learn from my experience, you may hear reason,
And never maim your fighting ; for your credit,
Which you think you have lost, spare Charles, and
        swinge me,
And soundly ; three or four walking velvet Cloaks,
That wear no swords to guard 'em, yet deserve it,
Thou art made up again.

EUST. All this is lip-salve.

MIR. It shall be hearts-ease, Eustace, ere I have
        done ;
As for thy father's anger, now thou dar'st fight,
Ne'er fear it, for I've the dowcets of his gravity
Fast in a string, I will so pinch and wring him,
That, spite of his authority, thou shalt make
Thine own conditions with him.

EUST. I'll take leave
A little to consider.

Enter ANDREW, *with his head broken.*

CHAR.   Here comes Andrew.

MIR.   But without his comical and learned face;
What sad disaster, Andrew?

AND.   You may read, sir,
A tragedy in my face.

MIR.   Art thou in earnest?

AND.   Yes, by my life, sir; and if now you help
      not,
And speedily, by force, or by persuasion,
My good old master (for now I pity him)
Is ruin'd for ever.

CHAR.   Ha, my father!

AND.   He, sir.

MIR.   By what means? speak.

AND.   At the suit of monsieur Lewis;
His house is seiz'd upon, and he in person
Is under guard, (I saw it with these eyes, Sir)
To be convey'd to Paris, and there sentenced.

MIR.   Nay, then there is no jesting.

CHAR.   Do I live,
And know my father injur'd?

AND.   And what's worse, sir,
My lady Angelina—

EUST.   What of her?

AND.   She's carried away too.

MIR.   How?

AND.   While you were absent,
A crew of monsieur Lewis' friends and kinsmen,
By force, brake in at th' back part of the house,

And took her away by violence ; faithful Andrew
(As this can witness for him) did his best
In her defence, but 'twould not do.

MIR.   Away,
And see our horses saddled, 'tis no time
To talk, but do. Eustace, you now are offer'd
A spacious field, and in a pious war
To exercise your valour ; here's a cause,
And such a one, in which to fall is honourable,
Your duty and reverence due to a father's name
Commanding it ; but these unnatural jars
Arising between brothers (should you prosper)
Would shame your victory.

EUST.   I would do much, sir,
But still my reputation !

MIR.   Charles shall give you
All decent satisfaction ; nay, join hands,
And heartily, why, this is done like brothers ;
And as old as I am, in this cause that concerns
The honour of our family, monsieur Lewis
(If reason cannot work) shall find and feel
There's hot blood in this arm, I'll lead you bravely.

EUST.   And if I follow not, a coward's name
Be branded on my forehead.

CHAR.   This spirit makes you
A sharer in my fortunes.

MIR.   And in mine,
Of which (Brisac once freed, and Angelina
Again in our possession) you shall know,
My heart speaks in my tongue.

EUST.   I dare not doubt it, sir.   [*Exeunt.*

SCENE II. *On high road to Paris.*

Enter LEWIS, BRISAC, ANGELINA, SYLVIA, *Officers.*

LEW. I'm deaf to all persuasions.

BRI.   I use none,
Nor doubt I, though a while my innocence suffers,
But when the king shall understand how false
Your malice hath inform'd him, he in justice
Must set me right again.

ANG.   Sir, let not passion
So far transport you, as to think in reason,
This violent course repairs, but ruins it ;
That honour you would build up, you destroy ;
What you would seem to nourish, if respect
Of my preferment or my pattern
May challenge your paternal love and care,
Why do you, now good fortune has provided
A better husband for me than your hopes
Could ever fancy, strive to rob me of him ?
In what is my lord Charles defective, sir ?
Unless deep learning be a blemish in him,
Or well proportion'd limbs be mulcts in nature,
Or, what you only aim'd at, large revenues,
Are, on the sudden, grown distasteful to you.
Of what can you accuse him ?

LEW.   Of a shame done to honour, which thy
            undutiful will
Made thee consent to.

SYL.   Were you ten lords, 'tis false ;
The pureness of her chaste thoughts entertains not
Such spotted instruments.

ANG. As I have a soul, sir,—

LEW. I am not to be alter'd; to sit down
With this disgrace, would argue me a peasant,
And not born noble: all rigour that the law,
And that increase of power by favour yields,
Shall be with all severity inflicted;
You have the king's hand for't, no bail will serve,
And therefore at your perils, officers,
Away with 'em.

BRI. This is madness.

LEW. Tell me so in open court,
And there I'll answer you.

Enter MIRAMONT, CHARLES, EUSTACE, ANDREW.

MIR. Well overtaken.

CHAR. Ill if they dare resist.

EUST. He that advances
But one step forward dies.

LEW. Shew the king's writ.

MIR. Shew your discretion, 'twill become you better.

CHAR. [*To Angelina.*] You are once more in my
power, and if again
I part with you, let me for ever lose thee.

EUST. Force will not do't, nor threats; accept this
service
From your despair'd of Eustace.

LEW. Is the king's power contemn'd?

MIR. No, but the torrent
O' your wilful folly stopp'd. And for you, good sir,
If you would but be sensible, what can you wish,
But the satisfaction of an obstinate will,
That is not endear'd to you? rather than

Be cross'd in what you purpos'd, you'll undo
Your daughter's fame, the credit of your judgment,
And your old foolish neighbour ; make your estates,
And in a suit not worth a cardecue[1],
A prey to advocates, and their buckram scribes,
And after they have plum'd you, return home
Like a couple of naked fowls without a feather.
  CHAR. This is a most strong truth, sir.
  MIR. No, no, monsieur,
Let us be right Frenchmen, violent to charge ;
But when our follies are repell'd by reason,
'Tis fit that we retreat, and ne'er come on more :
Observe my learned Charles, he'll bring thy daughter
      honour : and here's Eustace.
He was an ass, but now is grown an Amadis ;
Nor shall he want a wife, if all my land,
For a jointure, can effect : you are a good lord,
And of a gentle nature, in your looks
I see a kind consent, and it shews lovely :
And do you hear, old fool ?
[*To Brisac.*] But I'll not chide,
Hereafter, like me, ever doat on learning,
The mere belief is excellent, 'twill save you ;
And next, love valour, though you dare not fight
Your self, or fright a foolish officer, young Eustace
Can do it to a hair. And, to conclude,
Let Andrew's farm be increas'd.
So embrace on all sides.

    I'll pay those bilmen, and make large amends,
    Provided we preserve you still our friends—

                        [*Exeunt.*

[1] I.e. penny.

EPILOGUE

'Tis not the hands, or smiles, or common way
Of approbation to a well-liked Play,
We only hope ;—but that you freely would
To th' Author's memory so far unfold,
And show your loves and liking to his Wit,
Not in your praise, but often seeing it ;
That being the grand assurance that can give
The Poet and the Player means to live.

For EU product safety concerns, contact us at Calle de José Abascal, 56–1°,
28003 Madrid, Spain or eugpsr@cambridge.org.

www.ingramcontent.com/pod-product-compliance
Ingram Content Group UK Ltd.
Pitfield, Milton Keynes, MK11 3LW, UK
UKHW020312140625
459647UK00018B/1834